PRIVATE EYE
Colemanballs
15

D0293115

A selection of quotes,
most of which originally appeared
in PRIVATE EYE's
'Colemanballs' column.

Our thanks once again to all the readers
who sent us their contributions,
and to whom this book is dedicated.

PRIVATE EYE
Colemanballs
15

Compiled and edited by
BARRY FANTONI

Illustrated by
Bill Tidy

PRIVATE EYE

Published in Great Britain
by Private Eye Productions Ltd,
6 Carlisle Street, London W1D 3BN

© 2010 Pressdram Ltd
ISBN 1 901784 54 1
Designed by Bridget Tisdall
Printed in Great Britain by
Clays Ltd, St Ives plc

FSC
Mixed Sources
Product group from well-managed
forests and other controlled sources
Cert no. SGS-COC-2061
www.fsc.org
© 1996 Forest Stewardship Council

Athletics

"We could be getting a brace of medals by the end of the evening – in fact we could even get a couple."

BBC2

Boxing

"It wasn't a comeback. I always intended to come back."

BARRY McGUIGAN

"From when I was a baby, I said I would be the heavyweight world champion."

DAVID HAYE

I DON'T WANT NO HOLDING, GOUGING OR SHOUTING 'PUSH', OK?

"He [Nikolay Valuev] is a huge man. He's got arms like tree-trunks, his legs are like forests..."

DAVID SMITH

Cookery

"If your fridge is full this Christmas, use nature's refrigerator – your car!"

ANTHEA TURNER

"So, before you were vegetarian, did you eat meat?"

JUMOKE FASHOLA

"I think that I've got an awful lot of potential still to come."

CONTESTANT, MASTERCHEF

"...I think I'm anally tidy..."

CONTESTANT, COME DINE WITH ME

"...they are in-between No Man's Land..."
RAYMOND BLANC

"I'm just concentrating. I can't even think right now."
JANE MIDDLEMISS, MASTERCHEF

Cricket

"They've now played one, won one and lost one as well."
GARY RICHARDSON

"Gee, he looks like Moses. Where's his Ark?"
DEAN JONES

"The crowd are buzzing like new birds in a nest."

CHRISTOPHER MARTIN-JENKINS

"It's a simple complicated technique being displayed here."

MICHAEL ATHERTON

"I expect both teams to win the toss and bat."

MICHAEL VAUGHAN

"Sometimes you've got no choice where you're born."

GEOFFREY BOYCOTT

"He's [Andrew Strauss] not afraid to shirk the issues there."

ANGUS FRASER

"And, finally, Johnson gets umpire Koertzen's finger up..."

CHRISTOPHER MARTIN-JENKINS

"We don't want to over-egg the goose."

KEITH ANDREWS

"There's a certain symmetry to his figures:
4-3-2-1..."

GERALD DE KOCK

"He tried to cut off his nose in spite of his face."
MATTHEW HAYDEN

"The Australians don't seem to have the wind
beneath their belts."

MATTHEW HOGGARD

"England really need to bring some impotence into the attack."

MATTHEW HOGGARD

"Hussey was struggling to come to terms with the vagrancies in the wicket."

PAUL ALLOTT

"I don't believe in miracles. The last one I saw was in 1981."

GEOFFREY BOYCOTT

"This will be the death knell in the coffin of Pakistani cricket."

CHRIS BROAD

"I only watch the replays afterwards."

GEOFFREY BOYCOTT

"We mustn't sit on our laurels..."

MIKE GATTING

"These players are under the thumb of the microscope."

PHIL TUFNELL

"He'll put the wind up you when he gets the bit between his tail."

GEOFFREY BOYCOTT

"Not an easy catch but, equally, not a difficult catch."

MARK NICHOLAS

"Kent won eleven games unbeaten."

CHRIS ADAMS

"They have got a couple of big guns who can put them to the sword."

RONNIE IRANI

"Botham talks about Brearley in glowing tongues."

JIMMY TARBUCK

"It is time for us to nail our colours to our chests."

ANDREW STRAUSS

"I took great solstice from England's Ashes win."

MARTIN ADAMS

"The responsibility has been thrust very firmly on my door."

ANDREW STRAUSS

"Normally, the Pakistani police have rifles and atomic weapons."

GEOFFREY BOYCOTT

"I'd forgotten how they mentally think..."
GEOFFREY BOYCOTT

"Jonathan Powell has two of the longest pairs of legs in Test Cricket."
CHRISTOPHER MARTIN-JENKINS

Cycling

"Two Spanish flags for the crowd to see – one of them Japanese..."

CARLTON KIRBY

Dancing

"The highlight for me was when the top came off and you realised what a lovely pair they were."

LEN GOODMAN

Darts

"It's going to plummet him way up the rankings."

ALAN WARRINER-LITTLE

Football

"Looks like Portsmouth have thrown the white flag into the ring."

STAN COLLYMORE

"Spurs are a democracy now, with Harry Redknapp the dictator at the top."

DAVID PLEAT

"The journalists will be sharpening their pens."
ANDY HINCHCLIFFE

"There are no degrees of anger, no scale: when he [Alex Ferguson] loses his temper, he loses his temper – force 10."

ANDY COLE

"I've just had a slurp of warm tea that Danny [Mills] brought up at half-time."

JOHN MURRAY

"The pitch out there has been totally two-faced."
PHIL THOMPSON

"They [Wolverhampton Wanderers] were hanging on for grim death..."
ALAN HANSEN

"...then Rooney scored after a fluid exchange with Giggs..."
SIMON BROTHERTON

"It's one of those oblong balls, and it's in his area."

STEVE CLARIDGE

"The great thing about Campbell is his work ethic. No defender can rest when he's breathing down their shoulders."

ALAN SMITH

"You try to put your body between yourself and the ball..."

EIDUR GUDJOHNSEN

"Anelka was deliberately brought down in the box... anywhere else on the pitch and it would have been a penalty!"

SCOTT BOOT

"So Harry – is this a game Tottenham must win or is it a game you can't afford to lose?"

SETANTA SPORTS

"Terry got the deciding goal in Chelsea's 2-0 victory over Stoke."

BBC RADIO DEVON

"He has to start a little bit better than he has already begun..."

DAVID PLEAT

"He had to turn and swivel at the same time."

CHRIS KAMARA

"Fulham attack, but a host of green-shirted legs are in the way!"

BBC RADIO LONDON

"His arm was a long way from his body..."

PETER DRURY

"He [Robinho] is passing the ball like an expensive plate of mince pies."

DAVE MILLS

"Alex McLeish is having thoughts inside his head..."

GARETH SOUTHGATE

"Another mumbo-jumbo of a goalmouth there."

DAVID PLEAT

"There's no argument, he's [Anelka] arguably in the form of his life."

MARK LAWRENSON

"We just want to get ready for next week when the whistle really starts."

TONY PULIS

"...He [Fletcher] is an industrial player..."

JIMMY ARMFIELD

"I don't know any footballer whose legs have come back..."

MARK LAWRENSON

"How do you get your two best midfielders to play well together? Capello, unlike his successors, has the answer."

JAMIE REDKNAPP

"If you look at the harsh reality of football, if you want to win a match then you've got to score a goal."

IAN McGARRY

"They (Northwich Victoria) are rattling a few of Charlton's feathers."

ANDY TOWNSEND

"Celtic's Garry Caldwell is enjoying a miserable few weeks at the start of the season."

IAN CROCKER

"Last year in the Carling Cup against Arsenal, Tottenham came out of the traps like a house on fire."

ALAN SMITH

"It [a penalty decision] is one that could have gone either way – and did!"

CLIVE TYLDESLEY

"They [Valladolid] went on to lose that game quite comfortably in the end."

TERRY GIBSON

"Never has a football club the size of Saints in recent history really had to stare into the precipice."

NICK ILLINGSWORTH

"You can never say never, unless you say never yourself."

EMILE HESKEY

"Roy Keane: a personification of himself, in a way."

MATT JACKSON

"...and Stewie Downing will look at this with his left foot."

GARY GILL

"Swindon are collapsing around their own ears."
BBC RADIO LONDON

"He's an interesting player – short back legs..."
DAVID PLEAT

"The whole transformation of the game has just turned."
TEDDY SHERINGHAM

"He's not a lad that likes to stand on his feet..."
CHRIS WADDLE

"There were no questions asked when Michael Owen was taken off. 55 seconds later all the questions were answered when Martins scored."
SKY SPORTS NEWS

"Bobby Moore always had his suits manicured."
JAMIE REDKNAPP

" ...a lot of teams play each other towards the end of the season."
MICK QUINN

"You know sometimes football turns on the
slightest biscuit of good fortune."

DAVID PLEAT

"I'm sure they [Spurs] will get another opportunity, hopefully before the final whistle."

STEVE CLARIDGE

"Best team won, no complaints. But I thought their first goal was offside."

ALAN SHEARER

"Ronaldo can pull anything out of the hat at the drop of a whim."

PAUL MASEFIELD

"England are learning to walk before they can run with their feet nailed firmly to the ground."

CLIVE TYLDESLEY

"He [Roque Santa Cruz] doesn't look one million per cent happy."

ANDY GRAY

"You'd need Medusa to predict that..."

CHARLIE NICHOLAS

"Viewers in some regions were still able to
see substitute Dan Gosling's goal just seconds
before it happened..."

BBC NEWS WEBSITE

"You can't beat everyone up all the time with the
same brush."

STEVE CLARIDGE

"They [Liverpool] would have been much closer
to where they are now if he [Anelka] had still
been there."

MARK LAWRENSON

"And so it's two down and three to go as
Manchester United aim for the quadruple."

IAN ABRAHAMS

"Possession [of the ball] is now nine-tenths of
the law."

DAVID PLEAT

"When you've got a mountain to climb you may
as well throw everything into the kitchen sink
straight away."

DAVID PLATT

"It's going to take time for Tony Adams to inflict his style of play on Portsmouth."

STAN COLLYMORE

"He was outstanding from the first minute to the second."

ROBERTO MARTINEZ

"The ECB have obviously been listening to us going at each other leather and tongs this morning."

MIKE PARRY

"Aliadière, the Frenchman with the never-ending name."

ITV

"It's Real Madrid, the antichrist."

MARK LAWRENSON

"There are a lot of tired legs in those white shirts."

ANDY GRAY

"If they can erect memorials to ex-players then I'm an adversary for one for Bobby Robson."

IAN HOLLOWAY

"Jesus Navas... nobody gets on the end of his cross."

SKY SPORTS

"Gilberto Silva: does exactly what it says on the tin."

CLIVE TYLDESLEY, ITV

"I was born in Johannesburg, South Africa at a very young age."

CRAIG JOHNSTON

"If you gave those [free kicks] all the time, you'd be giving them constantly."

PETER CROUCH

"I fear for Hull now. They are the downfall of their own loss."

DANNY MILLS

"He [Robbie Keane] was like the cat that got the cheese."

STAN COLLYMORE

"You can't win in football unless you win."

TONY MOWBRAY

"I'd rather lose if we're playing to win..."

IAN HOLLOWAY

"In the second half the tide turned completely on its head..."

RADIO 5 LIVE

"The goal was scored one minute before half time in the first half."

DAVID PLEAT

"I've never been so certain about anything in my life. I want to be a coach. Or a manager. I'm not sure which…"

PHIL NEVILLE

"Zola can relieve himself now he's 3-0 up."

CHARLIE NICHOLAS

"... and the Celtic supporters, holding their heads in their faces..."

DAVID BEGG

"You can get across a last-minute message to your team in the last half-hour or hour before the game."

GRAHAM TAYLOR

"There's no one to blame – they are just individual mistakes."

DAVID BECKHAM

"Free kick to Preston... just how fatal will it be for Liverpool?"

CLIVE TYLDESLEY

"The goalkeeper – his left hand just disintegrated."

PETER BEAGRIE

"This free-kick is going to be a left or a right-footed strike."

GERRY ARMSTRONG

"I'm sure you'll have a field day in December, come January."

TONY ADAMS

"Just to remind you, away goals don't count at all in the play offs."

IAN DARKE

"When we play at home in the Champions League the fans do expect at least three points."

SHAUN MOLONEY

"I didn't know it was going to happen and I've been proved right."

BLACKPOOL VERSUS CARDIFF

"Andy Cole has a trophy full of medals."

IAN WRIGHT

"The foot's on the other shoe."

BRENDAN RODGERS

"We've been hit by a tornado, from our own submarine."

KAREN BRADY

"There are as many questions as there are answers."

PETER DRURY

"Certainly, some of the Rangers bench were unanimous..."

BILLY DODDS

"He's certainly a man who knows his own man..."

MARK LAWRENSON

"I don't know what state of mind his body is in."

JAMIE REDKNAPP

"The toe is the Achilles' heel of the foot."

RON JAWORSKI

"We scored three goals at home and ninety-nine times out of ten that'll be enough."

DEAN WHITE

"Confidence seems to be draining away. You can invisibly see that."

MICHAEL OWEN

"They've got to stop this runaway train at the top of the football tree."

DAVID PLEAT

THEY'RE HAPPY.. CALL IT A DRAW!

"If there is a goal now, it's really going to go for the side that scores it."

GRAHAM TAYLOR

"Chelsea have five or six injured players out at the moment and if Ashley Cole is injured that makes it seven or eight..."

GLENN HODDLE

"They all looked around scratching each other's head."

GERRY ARMSTRONG

"This has been a perennial problem for many years."

DAVID PLEAT

"The manager is going to have to get the squad together and put the seeds of doubt to bed."

ALAN SMITH

"Martin [O'Neill] should be keeping young players' heads on the ground."

ALAN GREEN

"This league is strange, you can win one week and lose the next."

DAVID BECKHAM

"I'm neither decided nor undecided."

ROBBIE KEANE

"I'm sure they are going to make a couple of substitutions, probably off the bench."

DAVID PLEAT

"I don't want to swallow my words and eat them."

GARETH BARRY

"Stoke are throwing the Alamo at Liverpool at the moment."

STEVE HUNTER

"Everyone gave eight out of ten and you can't ask for any more than that."

PERRY GROVES

"At the end of the day, everyone starts somewhere."

JULIAN DICKS

"Eduardo will be making his comeback tonight after his fatal injury."

RADIO 5 LIVE

"He's worked his legs off."

LEE DIXON

"They have lots of multi-national players from all over the world."

MARTIN KEOWN

"Baptista, 27 years old. Late twenties? Early twenties."

DAVID PLEAT

"Tonight he's not had a kick other than two headers."

ROBBIE SAVAGE

"That finish was cool, calm and personified."

JOHN CHAMPION

"Of course mistakes are made – some are even accidental."

GRAHAM TAYLOR

"That pass wasn't meant for him... you can tell by the shape of the ball."

MARK LAWRENSON

"His [Gerrard's] first touch was perfect. His second even better..."

ANDY TOWNSEND

"His head's the wrong way round."

ALAN SHEARER

"There's going to be a goal any minute... at one end or the other."

CLIVE TYLDESLEY

"You wouldn't want to be a left-handed player for Japan, would you?"

MARK LAWRENSON

"That's what he's so adept at – just narrowly missing the target."

DEREK RAE

"...and England are all playing in red."

GUY MOWBRAY

"It's a probability: there's no doubt about that."
GRAHAM TAYLOR

"The only way you can win as a manager or coach, is to win."
MICK McCARTHY

"England can win the World Cup. If, on the day, they beat the opposition."
ROBBIE SAVAGE

"The keeper has gone with his correct hand because it's his nearest."
KEVIN KEEGAN

"Uruguay is a country of 3 million people and half of them are probably women."
RAY WILKINS

"We've got to go home, sort ourselves out, get fit, and come back next year."
JOHN TERRY

"He's used Heitinga as a target to miss."
KEVIN KEEGAN

"Aston Villa attacking their 1000-plus fans behind the goal..."

ITV

"We're either brilliant or useless in England, no in-between. We've had two average performances."

ALAN SHEARER

"It looked a little bit worse than it appeared..."

DAVID PLEAT

"And Domenech only has one more throw of the dice up his sleeve."

BBC 1

"Once he opens those big legs he can bc a handful."

CRAIG BURLEY

"With a name like Bravo he's either going to be brilliant or terrible."

ADRIAN CHILES

"The ball is unpredictable, but not all the time."

GLEN JOHNSTON

"The future isn't about yesterday – it's about today."

DAVID PLEAT

"He's got bags of legs."

ANDY TOWNSEND

"He was like a swan there – flying through the air, but no real quality at the end."

MARTIN KEOWN

Golf

"...the return of the Tiger – he was up and down, in and out, as usual."

PETER ALISS

"It was as if Faldo was trying to reinvent the wheel and put people in spokes that just didn't fit them."

DAVID FACEY

"That could be a harbinger of things to come."

MASTERS GOLF TOURNAMENT

"90% of putts that are short tend not to go in [the hole]."

SKY SPORTS

Horses

"He had a winner at the Curragh yesterday, that's the Newmarket of France."

DEREK THOMPSON

"The best horse won, and that's all you can ask in any sport..."

JOHN INVERDALE

"Jason McGuire takes a look between his legs and likes what he sees."

DEREK THOMPSON

"We have to remember that horses are only human..."

MIKE TUCKER

"I'm looking at that ice cream van over there and wondering how much they charge for a 69...?"

CORNELIUS LYSAGHT

Literally

"Cars have literally been in your blood since..."

ANGELA RIPPON

"They [Andorra] are literally going to park the bus on this one."

DAVID PLEAT

"The Royal Mail has been literally sinking into the ground."

CHERYL GILLAN

"He has literally thrown the kitchen sink at that delivery."

SHAUN UDAL

"Barcelona have promised their fans they will quite literally play out of their skins tonight."

CLIVE TYLDESLEY

"My legs literally turned to jelly."

RACHEL STEVENS

"Robinho has been literally non-existent..."

LEE DIXON

"I'd never danced before. I've literally got two left feet."

CHRISTINE BLEAKLEY

"It has literally been a plague on all our houses."

ANTHONY LITTLE

"Everyone in Israel is literally glued to their radio and television sets."

RADIO SCOTLAND NEWS

"England should literally put Algeria to bed."
ANDY TOWNSEND

"...you were up against the Norwegians who are, literally, born on skis."
KATE SILVERTON

"A wonderful David James save, literally in the dying embers of the game."

JEFF STELLING

"Let's hope we can keep the Ashes now... last time we literally fell apart."

ASHLEY GILES

"The Lib Dem leader has been literally squashed by the First Minister [Alex Salmond]."

KIT FRASER

"He [Damiano Cunego] literally tore the legs off his teammate, Gilberto Simoni, in the 2004 Giro d'Italia."

DAVID HARMON

"Gazza will literally be going through cold turkey for the rest of his life."

TALKSPORT

"He [Zaheer Khan] is literally making the ball talk..."

ARUN LAL

IF YOU HAVE DIFFICULTY UNDERSTANDING URDU I WILL INTERPRET...

"This new ball... literally explodes off the player's foot."

JAMIE REDKNAPP

"He [Michael Martin] should, quite literally, fall on his sword."

JOHN STONBOROUGH

"You can literally get a world on your plate."

JAMIE OLIVER

"And that goal has quite literally set the Stade Vélodrome on fire."

CLIVE TYLDESLEY

"If you're a Service family, my heart literally goes out to you."

SARAH KENNEDY

"We are literally the next cab off the block..."

SEBASTIAN COE

"They [Coventry] scored with the last throw of the dice – literally."

KEVIN KEEGAN

"They've literally got no players left – and then with 95 minutes gone they score."

LEE DIXON

"[Jamie Cullum] literally lives in a house made of records."

RADIO 2

"He [Jermaine Defoe] was just literally on fire..."
RADIO 5 LIVE

"It's different when you see Gerrard literally pick them up by the scruff of the neck and do it on his own."

IAN WRIGHT

"... it sounds like Lenin will be literally cheering in his grave."

JUSTIN WEBB

"This bunch of politicians are literally falling apart."

DAVID CAMERON

"In football they change their manager literally by the day..."

GARY RICHARDSON

"Vulnerable children in Doncaster are buried, quite literally, in a pile of paperwork."

DONCASTER SOCIAL SERVICES SPOKESPERSON

"Andy Johnson was literally banjoed out of the game by a player who made no attempt to win the ball."

ROY HODGSON

"On the Lions tour in 1997 Mark Regan and Barry Williams blew up, but it was literally handbags."

JEREMY GUSCOTT

Motor Sport

"Qualifying doesn't always tell us who has the quickest car, just who has the fastest car."

JAKE HUMPHREY

Music

"Your body has a mind of its own..."

ALESHA DIXON

"That's the kind of song that young kids know, even if they haven't heard it before."
STEVE WRIGHT SHOW

"It went global and then it went round the world..."
TWO-TONE MUSIC FAN, BBC MIDLANDS TODAY

Oddballs

"My thanks and commiserations to the other contestants, and to you for listening."
RUSSELL BRAND

"Is it your sister or brother who's his dad?"
VICTORIA DERBYSHIRE

"11am heralded 2 minutes silence that was echoed all over the country..."
BBC RADIO 4

"During her imprisonment, she gave birth to two girls aged 11 and 15."
SHAUN LEY

"This is knitting while Rome burns."

YASMIN ALIBHAI-BROWN

"This guy's a pathological homeopathic murderer."

RADIO 5 LIVE

"They have turned Parliament Square into a toilet. We have a big job on our hands..."

SIR SIMON MILTON

"The Notting Hill carnival is unrivalled, second only to the one at Rio."

CORRIE CORFIELD

"He has been the victim of his own downfall."

DC DAVID BEBB

"He is in fact being released to die – something which should have happened years ago."

RONNIE BIGGS'S SOLICITOR

"The incredible is always hard to believe."

SUPT ANTHONY McWHIRTER

"He had a small cut behind his ear, which at first I thought might be a head injury."

HENDON & FINCHLEY TIMES

"[There's] bound to be a deeply beating heart inside that young brain."

BILL LESLIE

"These are unprecedented scenes we haven't seen in years."

MIRANDA SCHUNKE

"Are they putting their finger on the nail here?"

SHELAGH FOGARTY

"Traffic is very sluggish in Stratford, due to the sheer weight of people."

RADIO COVENTRY & WARWICKSHIRE

"It's been a year of birthdays."

CLAIRE WHITAKER

"Very unusually, it has turned noon here in Washington."

HUW EDWARDS

"Have you got your feet firmly under the carpet now?"

HOLLY WILLOUGHBY

"Because Mr Madoff is 75, he will not be able to serve his whole 150 years service."

BBC NEWS 24

"The banks have made people green with anger over the last few years."

EVAN DAVIS

"My heart goes out to everyone awaiting an organ transplant."

ELIZABETH BUGGINS

"Gritters will be working around the clock for the next few hours."

BBC SCOTLAND NEWS

"It's hard to put my thoughts in their shoes."

ALEX GRAY

"...putting their snouts in the gravy train..."

DAME ANN LESLIE

"To me, that's a lack of impatience."

JOE JOHNSON

"Our hands are completely ham strung..."

RADIO 5 LIVE

"Did your great-grandfather have any children?"

FERN BRITTON

"So the obvious answer is 'why?'"

JOHN HUMPHRYS

"You can't teach an old leopard new spots."
                                    WIFE SWAP, CHANNEL 4

"He was a wonderful man, as was his wife."
                                    SEAN RAFFERTY

"He rubbed a few noses up the wrong way..."
                                    SIMON MAYO

Politics

"...if you are a widow, for whatever reason..."
                                    ED BALLS

"Every time I visit Iraq or Afghanistan I am
blown away..."

                                    DAVID CAMERON

"It's not a referendum any more, it's a choice."
                                    GORDON BROWN

"I am not a man of faith, but my wife is."
                                    NICK CLEGG

"It's passed on, like a Christmas tree, from person to person."

JOHN PRESCOTT

"Some of this stuff is political with Max Mosley. I mean, some people use the story as a stick to beat him with..."

NICKY CAMPBELL

"Obama can't be himself because of who he is. But now he is who he is."

BONNIE GREER

"I plot my own route through fate."

MIKE PARRY

"We are looking at legacy and legacy is about tomorrow..."

BRIAN MAWHINNEY

"Some people want Europe to be a retiring violet."

DAVID MILIBAND

"Funding is to be cut for sports where targets were missed, such as archery."

RADIO 5 LIVE

"...in particular China and India – I'm not singling them out."

ED MILIBAND

"Knives do more harm than good."

GORDON BROWN

"We went to university together, but not at the same time."

KEITH VAZ

"Let's not take our bridges before they've been erected."

BOB AINSWORTH

"He [Nick Griffin] did a great job of hanging himself by his own petard."

MIDGE URE

"Next we have someone who is following in her father's footsteps by becoming the first Asian female councillor in Rushmoor."

NICK WALLIS

"...when the PM saw this immovable object [Joanna Lumley] coming at a hundred miles an hour towards him..."

KEITH VAZ

"We should allow those who have sacrificed their lives for this country to come and live in this country."

SIR NICHOLAS WINTERTON

"If we're going to send people out to die for their country, then we're going to give them the equipment they need."

JEREMY HUNT

"The European Parliament seems to be a place where politicians go to milk the gravy train."

BBC WORLD SERVICE

"Heath Ledger looks a dead cert to be nominated for a posthumous Oscar award."

PETER BOWES

"The Government's going to kill the golden goose."

TIM MARTIN

"The Government wants all homes to be energy-efficient; that's a lofty ambition by 2020."

DEREK LICKORISH

"I think savers have got the short end of the stick..."

LYNNE FEATHERSTONE

"A lot of people have the political knife out and they're gunning for him."

JOHN RAINES

"That is not just a legacy, it is there for the future."

ALEX SALMOND

"No one is guilty until proved otherwise."

LORD WINSTON

"Liberalism with a small 'c'."

DAVID BLUNKETT

"All these eastern Europeans that are coming in – where are they flocking from?"

GILLIAN DUFFY

Question & Answer

PAUL HAYES (expert): So is this a family heirloom?

PARTICIPANT (dismissively): Noooo. It was my Gran's and she passed it on to my Mum who passed it on to me...

CAR BOOTY, BBC1

LOUISE MINCHIN: What is it like to have Sir Cliff Richard promoting this project?

ALZHEIMER SOCIETY SPOKESWOMAN: Well, dementia has been in the shadows for a long time...

SUNDAY LIFE

Rugby

"He plucked the ball out of the air like a salmon."

RAY FRENCH

"The whirligig of time brings round its revenges."

MILE HARRISON

"For the last ten minutes we've all been on the edge of our feet..."

MATT DAWSON, RADIO 5

"With the quality of the teams in this tournament, it's hard to imagine that somebody won't beat somebody else, at some stage."

DENNIS HICKEY

"You don't have to be a rocket surgeon to know that you need to get up quick on him."

BARRY McDERMOTT

"Brian Moore got [drug] tested after every single game in the World Cup and it got up his nose..."

JEREMY GUSCOTT

"...and Wasps travel to Bath for a fixture that rarely fails to disappoint."

SKY SPORTS NEWS

"It's bad for the wives, sitting on the side watching your husband go down."

MRS JOHANN MULLER

"England are looking down the barrel of a yellow card..."

BRIAN MOORE

"The defence seemed to be caught in two man's land."

EDDIE HEMMINGS

Snooker

"You could visibly see him trying harder there as the frame went on. It might not have looked like it..."

JOHN PARROTT

"He's got his tail between his legs and a spring in his step."

CHRISTOPHER JOUBERT

"His title was hanging by a thin thread, and still is, as we go past the midnight hour, as Wilson Pickett would have said."

JOHN VIRGO

"At this stage of my career I regard any win as a result."

RONNIE O'SULLIVAN

"They'll all be crossing their fingers and their legs now."

JOHN VIRGO

"Well, John, I'd rather nearly win than nearly lose."

TERRY GRIFFITHS

Tennis

"That was pure instinct from Murray – made up his mind to go for that..."

JOHN LLOYD

"And he tucks that one away like a book of tennis unfolding in front of you."

BBC

"I'm currently writing a screenplay that I haven't started yet."

SERENA WILLIAMS

"Pete Sampras has just arrived. He has not been seen here since the last time he was here."

BORIS BECKER

"He's won three Grand Slams on three different occasions."

TIM HENMAN

"All the changing room'll have their feet off the floor."

DAVID LLOYD

"Simon is tying his shoelaces to the left of the umpire's chair."

JONATHAN OVEREND

"Winning matches is the best recipe for winning."

VIRGINIA WADE

"Yes, the wind is coming from Federer's end..."

BBC

"In tennis there has to be a winner sometimes."

ROGER FEDERER

"He's picking and choosing the shots that he's choosing."

ANDREW CASTLE

"I've been accused of a lot of shortcomings in my career, but trying hard isn't one of them."

ANDY RODDICK

"Laura Robson has just made the best possible start to her professional tennis career, she won the first set and lost the next two and is out."

MARK POUGATCH

"He managed to get himself a seat in the now vanished standing section of centre court."

SIMON BARNES

Women's Football

"The girls just have to hang their heads up high."
FAYE WHITE

"Prinz is arguably or indisputably the best player in the world."
GUY MOWBRAY

"Women's football does have its knockers."
ADRIAN DURHAM